No Lang

No Language Is Neutral

Dionne Brand

Coach House Press · Toronto

Published with the assistance of the Canada Council
and the Ontario Arts Council

'No Language Is Neutral' is from Derek Walcott's
Midsummer Lii.

Thanks to Ted Chamberlin for his advice and reading of this
work over the last year. Thanks also to Michael Ondaatje for
his support. Sisterhood to the Toronto Black Women's
Collective for listening to it.
Parts of the title poem appeared in *Brick,*
and in *Saturday Night.*
The first poem in 'hard against the soul' appeared in *Sight
Specific,* and in *Dykewords, An Anthology of Lesbian Writing.*

Canadian Cataloguing in Publication

Brand, Dionne
No language is neutral

Poems.
ISBN 0-88910-395-X

I. Title.
PS8553.R285N6 1990   C811'.54   C90-095281-4
PR9199.3.B736N6 1990

hard against the soul

I

this is you girl, this cut of road up
to blanchicheuse, this every turn a piece
of blue and earth carrying on, beating, rock and
ocean this wearing away, smoothing the insides
pearl of shell and coral

this is you girl, this is you all sides of me
hill road and dip through the coconut at manzanilla
this sea breeze shaped forest of sand and lanky palm
this wanting to fall, hanging, greening
quenching the road

this is you girl, even though you never see it
the drop before timberline, that daub of black shine
sea on bush smoke land, that pulse of the heart
that stretches up to maracas, la fillete bay never know
you but you make it wash up from the rocks

this is you girl, that bit of lagoon, alligator
long abandoned, this stone of my youngness
hesitating to walk right, turning to Schoener's road
turning to duenne and spirit, to the sea wall and sea
breaking hard against things, turning to burning reason

this is you girl, this is the poem no woman
ever write for a woman because she 'fraid to touch
this river boiling like a woman in she sleep
that smell of fresh thighs and warm sweat
sheets of her like the mitan rolling into the atlantic

this is you girl, something never waning or forgetting
something hard against the soul
this is where you make sense, that the sight becomes
tender, the night air human, the dull silence full
chattering, volcanoes cease, and to be awake is
more lovely than dreams

Return

return

I

So the street is still there, still melting with sun
still the shining waves of heat at one o'clock
the eyelashes scorched, staring the distance of the
park to the parade stand, still razor grass burnt and
cropped, everything made indistinguishable from dirt
by age and custom, white washed, and the people ...
still I suppose the scorpion orchid by the road, that
fine red tongue of flamboyant and orange lips
muzzling the air, that green plum turning fat and
crimson, still the crazy bougainvillea fancying and
nettling itself purple, pink, red, white, still the trickle of
sweat and cold flush of heat raising the smell of
cotton and skin ... still the dank rank of breadfruit milk,
their bash and rain on steps, still the bridge this side
the sea that side, the rotting ship barnacle eaten still
the butcher's blood staining the walls of the market,
the ascent of hills, stony and breathless, the dry
yellow patches of earth still threaten to swamp at the
next deluge ... so the road, that stretch of sand and
pitch struggling up, glimpses sea, village, earth
bare-footed hot, women worried, still the faces,
masked in sweat and sweetness, still the eyes
watery, ancient, still the hard, distinct, brittle smell of
slavery.

Phyllis

Phyllis, quite here, I hear from you
not even from your own hand in a note
but from some stranger who dragged it
from a prison wall, a letter running
like a karili vine around Richmond Hill
Phyllis, I know they treat you bad
like a woman
I know is you one there and I
never forget how one night you give
me a ride in your car
and I never forget your laugh like a bronze bauble
hanging in that revolutionary evening
Phyllis, when you sit down and explain
the revolution, it did sound sweet and it
did sound possible.

For Phyllis Coard
Minister of Women's Affairs in the People's Revolutionary
Gov't. of Grenada, 1979-1983, now imprisoned at Richmond
Hill Prison in Grenada for her role in a coup.

Phyllis, quite here, I hear how
you so thin now, but still strong
your voice refusing departures and
soldiers cursing, your voice ringing through
bars with messages to keep up the struggle
now buried in death bed and prison wall,
I know they treat you bad
like a woman
called you *hyena*, a name enjoining
you alone to biology and not science,
you should have known
the first thing they would jump on
was the skill of your womb
Phyllis, I remember your laugh, luminous
and bubbling in the flaming dark evening
and the moment after, your eyes serious,
searching for your glasses.

Girl, how come is quite here I hear from you,
sitting in these rooms, resenting this messenger,
out here, I listen through an upstart castigate
Fidel, scraping my chair to interrupt him,
just to see if you send any explanations,
I know they treat you bad
like a woman
you, bewitched in their male dramas,
their comess and their tay tay,
you, foundered, as Bernard said, in all
the usual last minute domestic things
a housewife has to do
Phyllis, they said you defied the prison guards
and talked through their shouts to be quiet
your laugh clanging against the stone walls
your look silencing soldiers.

Jackie

Jackie, that first evening I met you, you thought I was
a child to be saved from Vincent's joke, I was a
stranger in the room that your eyes vined like a
school teacher's folding me in, child, to be taken care
of. An afternoon on that grand beach you threw your
little boy among the rest of children in the hissing
ocean surf, dreaming an extraordinary life, an idea
fanning La Sagesse and Carib's Leap then slabs of
volcanic clay in a reddened ocean, perhaps even
larger. Jackie, gently, that glint of yellow in your eyes,
end of a day, cigarette smoke masking your tiredness
and impatience with this gratuitous rain of foreign
clerks, then you talked patiently, the past burning at
the back of your head. That day on the last hill, bright
midday heat glistened on your hands you were in
yellow too, yellow like fire on a cornbird's back, fire at
your mouth the colour of lightning, then in the last
moment, bullets crisscrossed your temple and your
heart. They say someone was calling you, Yansa,
thundering for help.

For Jacqueline Creft
Minister of Education in the People's Revolutionary
Gov't of Grenada, killed on October 19th. 1983
during a coup.

return

II

From here you can see Venezuela,
that is not Venezuela, girl, that is Pointe Galeote
right round the corner, is not away
over that sea swelling like a big belly woman
that must have been a look of envy

every eye looking out of its black face many years
ago must have longed to dive into the sea woman's
belly swimming to away only to find
Pointe Galeote's nubbly face
back to there and no further than the heat flush

every woman must have whispered
in her child's ear, away! far from here!
people go mad here walking into the sea!
the air sick, sibylline, away! go away!
crashing and returning against Pointe Galeote

From here envied tails of water swing out
and back playing sometimeish historian
covering hieroglyphs and naming fearsome artifacts,
That is not footsteps, girl, is duenne!
is not shell, is shackle!

Amelia still

Mama must have left then
that day when I hung out the window
and saw the drabness of the street
and felt that no one lived in the house
any longer, she must have carried herself off to the
bush, grabbed up her own ghost and ran all the way
to Toco, ran all the way out of the hell of us
tied to her breasts and sweeping her brain
for answers. Mama must have fled that day
when I noticed that her shadow
left the veranda and understood that sweet water was
only lyrical in a girl child's wild undertakings
she must have gone hunting for her heart
where she had dropped it as she buried each navel
string hunting, hunting her blood and milk
spread over our stained greedy faces.
Mama must have gone crazy
trying to wrench herself away
from my memory burning around her
and denying her the bread of her death
as food from her mouth
she must have hurried to the Ortoire river
to wash her own hair, take her sweet time
waking up, pitch stones over water,
eat a little sugar, in peace.

Blues Spiritual for Mammy Prater

On looking at 'the photograph of Mammy Prater an ex-slave,
115 years old when her photograph was taken'

she waited for her century to turn
she waited until she was one hundred and fifteen
years old to take a photograph
to take a photograph and to put those eyes in it
she waited until the technique of photography was
suitably developed
to make sure the picture would be clear
to make sure no crude daguerreotype would lose
her image
would lose her lines and most of all her eyes
and her hands
she knew the patience of one hundred and fifteen years
she knew that if she had the patience,
to avoid killing a white man
that I would see this photograph
she waited until it suited her
to take this photograph and to put those eyes in it.

in the hundred and fifteen years which it took her to
wait for this photograph she perfected this pose
she sculpted it over a shoulder of pain,
a thing like despair which she never called
this name for she would not have lasted
the fields, the ones she ploughed
on the days that she was a mule, left
their etching on the gait of her legs
deliberately and unintentionally
she waited, not always silently, not always patiently,
for this self portrait
by the time she sat in her black dress, white collar,
white handkerchief, her feet had turned to marble,
her heart burnished red,
and her eyes.

she waited one hundred and fifteen years
until the science of photography passed tin and
talbotype for a surface sensitive enough
to hold her eyes
she took care not to lose the signs
to write in those eyes what her fingers could not script
a pact of blood across a century, a decade and more
she knew then that it would be me who would find
her will, her meticulous account, her eyes,
her days when waiting for this photograph
was all that kept her sane
she planned it down to the day,
the light,
the superfluous photographer
her breasts,
her hands
this moment of
my turning the leaves of a book,
noticing, her eyes.

no language is neutral

No language is neutral. I used to haunt the beach at
Guaya, two rivers sentinel the country sand, not
backra white but nigger brown sand, one river dead
and teeming from waste and alligators, the other
rumbling to the ocean in a tumult, the swift undertow
blocking the crossing of little girls except on the tied
up dress hips of big women, then, the taste of leaving
was already on my tongue and cut deep into my
skinny pigeon toed way, language here was strict
description and teeth edging truth. Here was beauty
and here was nowhere. The smell of hurrying passed
my nostrils with the smell of sea water and fresh fish
wind, there was history which had taught my eyes to
look for escape even beneath the almond leaves fat
as women, the conch shell tiny as sand, the rock
stone old like water. I learned to read this from a
woman whose hand trembled at the past, then even
being born to her was temporary, wet and thrown half
dressed among the dozens of brown legs itching to
run. It was as if a signal burning like a fer de lance's
sting turned my eyes against the water even as love
for this nigger beach became resolute.

There it was anyway, some damn memory half-eaten
and half hungry. To hate this, they must have been
dragged through the Manzinilla spitting out the last
spun syllables for cruelty, new sound forming,
pushing toward lips made to bubble blood. This road
could match that. Hard-bitten on mangrove and wild
bush, the sea wind heaving any remnants of
consonant curses into choking aspirate. No
language is neutral seared in the spine's unravelling.
Here is history too. A backbone bending and
unbending without a word, heat, bellowing these
lungs spongy, exhaled in humming, the ocean, a
way out and not anything of beauty, tipping turquoise
and scandalous. The malicious horizon made us the
essential thinkers of technology. How to fly gravity,
how to balance basket and prose reaching for
murder. Silence done curse god and beauty here,
people does hear things in this heliconia peace
a morphology of rolling chain and copper gong
now shape this twang, falsettos of whip and air
rudiment this grammar. Take what I tell you. When
these barracks held slaves between their stone
halters, talking was left for night and hush was idiom
and hot core.

When Liney reach here is up to the time I hear about. Why I always have to go back to that old woman who wasn't even from here but from another barracoon, I never understand but deeply as if is something that have no end. Even she daughter didn't know but only leave me she life like a brown stone to see. I in the middle of a plane ride now a good century from their living or imagination, around me is a people I will only understand as full of ugliness that make me weep full past my own tears and before hers. Liney, when she live through two man, is so the second one bring she here on his penultimate hope and she come and sweep sand into my eye. So is there I meet she in a recollection through Ben, son, now ninety, ex-saga boy and image, perhaps eyes of my mama, Liney daughter. I beg him to recall something of my mama, something of his mama. The ninety year old water of his eyes swell like the river he remember and he say, *she was a sugar cake, sweet sweet sweet. Yuh muma! that girl was a sugar cake!*

This time Liney done see vision in this green guava
season, fly skinless and turn into river fish, dream
sheself, praise god, without sex and womb when sex
is hell and womb is she to pay. So dancing an old
man the castilian around this christmas living room
my little sister and me get Ben to tell we any story he
remember, and in between his own trail of conquests
and pretty clothes, in between his never sleeping with
a woman who wasn't clean because he was a
scornful man, in between our absent query were they
scornful women too, Liney smiled on his gold teeth.
the castilian out of breath, the dampness of his
shrunken skin reminding us, Oh god! laughing,
sister! we will kill uncle dancing!

In between, Liney, in between , as if your life could
never see itself, blooded and coarsened on this
island as mine, driven over places too hard to know
in their easy terror. As if your life could never hear
itself as still some years, god, ages, have passed
without your autobiography now between my stories
and the time I have to remember and the passages
that I too take out of liking, between me and history
we have made a patch of it, a verse still missing you
at the subject, a chapter yellowed and moth eaten at
the end. I could never save a cactus leaf between
pages, Liney, those other girls could make them root
undisturbed in the steam of unread books, not me,
admiring their devotion, still I peered too often at my
leaf, eyeing the creeping death out of it and giving up.
That hovel in the cocoa near the sweet oil factory I'll
never see, Liney, each time I go I stand at the road
arguing with myself. Sidelong looks are my specialty.
That saddle of children given you by one man then
another, the bear and darn and mend of your vagina
she like to walk about plenty, Ben said, *she was a
small woman, small small*. I chase Ben's romance as
it mumbles to a close, then, the rum and cocunut
water of his eyes as he prepares to lie gently for his
own redemption. *I was she favourite, oh yes.*
The ric rac running of your story remains braided in
other wars, Liney, no one is interested in telling the
truth. History will only hear you if you give birth to a
woman who smoothes starched linen in the wardrobe
drawer, trembles when she walks and who gives birth
to another woman who cries near a river and
vanishes and who gives birth to a woman who is a
poet, and, even then.

Pilate was that river I never crossed as a child. A
woman, my mother, was weeping on its banks,
weeping for the sufferer she would become, she a too
black woman weeping, those little girls trailing her
footsteps reluctantly and without love for this shaking
woman blood and salt in her mouth, weeping, that
river gushed past her feet blocked her flight ... and go
where, lady, weeping and go where, turning back to
face herself now only the oblique shape of something
without expectation, her body composed in doubt
then she'd come to bend her back, to dissemble, then
to stand on anger like a ledge, a tilting house, the
crazy curtain blazing at her teeth. A woman who
though she was human but got the message, female
and black and somehow those who gave it to her
were like family, mother and brother, spitting woman
at her, somehow they were the only place to return to
and this gushing river had already swallowed most of
her, the little girls drowned on its indifferent bank, the
river hardened like the centre of her, spinning chalk
stone on its frill, burden in their slow feet, they
weeping, she, *go on home,* in futility. There were
dry-eyed cirri tracing the blue air that day. Pilate was
that river I ran from leaving that woman, my mother,
standing over its brutal green meaning and it was
over by now and had become so ordinary as if not to
see it any more, that constant veil over the eyes, the
blood-stained blind of race and sex.

Leaving this standing, heart and eyes fixed to a skyscraper and a concrete eternity not knowing then only running away from something that breaks the heart open and nowhere to live. Five hundred dollars and a passport full of sand and winking water, is how I reach here, a girl's face shimmering from a little photograph, her hair between hot comb and afro, feet posing in high heel shoes, never to pass her eyes on the red-green threads of a humming bird's twitching back, the blood warm quickened water colours of a sea bed, not the rain forest tangled in smoke-wet, well there it was. I did read a book once about a prairie in Alberta since my waving canefield wasn't enough, too much cutlass and too much cut foot, but romance only happen in romance novel, the concrete building just overpower me, block my eyesight and send the sky back, back where it more redolent.

Is steady trembling I trembling when they ask me my
name and say I too black for it. Is steady hurt I feeling
when old talk bleed, the sea don't have branch you
know darling. Nothing is a joke no more and I right
there with them, running for the train until I get to find
out my big sister just like to run and nobody wouldn't
vex if you miss the train, calling Spadina *Spadeena*
until I listen good for what white people call it, saying I
coming just to holiday to the immigration officer when
me and the son-of a bitch know I have labourer mark
all over my face. It don't have nothing call beauty
here but this is a place, a gasp of water from a
hundred lakes, fierce bright windows screaming with
goods, a constant drizzle of brown brick cutting
dolorous prisons into every green uprising of bush.
No wilderness self, is shards, shards, shards,
shards of raw glass, a debris of people you pick your way
through returning to your worse self, you the thin
mixture of just come and don't exist.

I walk Bathurst Street until it come like home
Pearl was near Dupont, upstairs a store one
christmas where we pretend as if nothing change we,
make rum punch and sing, with bottle and spoon,
song we weself never even sing but only hear when
we was children. Pearl, squeezing her big Point
Fortin self along the narrow hall singing *Drink a rum
and a ...* Pearl, working nights, cleaning, Pearl beating
books at her age, Pearl dying back home in a car
crash twenty years after everything was squeezed in,
a trip to Europe, a condominium, a man she suckled
like a baby. Pearl coaxing this living room with a
voice half lie and half memory, a voice no room
nowhere could believe was sincere. Pearl hoping this
room would catch fire above this frozen street. Our
singing parched, drying in the silence after the
chicken and ham and sweet bread effort to taste like
home, the slim red earnest sound of long ago with the
blinds drawn and the finally snow for christmas and
the mood that rum in a cold place takes. Well, even
our nostalgia was a lie, skittish as the truth these
bundle of years.

But wait, this must come out then. A hidden verb
takes inventory of those small years like a person
waiting at a corner, counting and growing thin
through life as cloth and as water, hush ... Look I
hated something, policemen, bankers, slavetraders,
shhh ... still do and even more these days. This city,
mourning the smell of flowers and dirt , cannot tell
me what to say even if it chokes me. Not a single
word drops from my lips for twenty years about living
here. Dumbfounded I walk as if these sidewalks are a
place I'm visiting. Like a holy ghost, I package the
smell of zinnias and lady of the night, I horde the taste
of star apples and granadilla. I return to that once
grammar struck in disbelief. Twenty years. Ignoring
my own money thrown on the counter, the race
conscious landlords and their jim crow flats, oh yes!
here! the work nobody else wants to do ... it's good
work I'm not complaining! but they make it taste bad,
bitter like peas. You can't smile here, is a sin, you
can't play music, it too loud. There was a time I could
tell if rain was coming, it used to make me sad the
yearly fasting of trees here, I felt some pity for the
ground turned hot and cold. All that time taken up
with circling this city in a fever. I remember then, and
it's hard to remember waiting so long to live ... anyway
it's fiction what I remember, only mornings took a long
time to come, I became more secretive, language
seemed to split in two, one branch fell silent, the other
argued hotly for going home.

This is the part that is always difficult, the walk each night across the dark school yard, biting my tongue on new english, reading biology, stumbling over unworded white faces. But I am only here for a moment. The new stink of wet wool, driving my legs across snow, ice, counting the winters that I do not skid and fall on, a job sorting cards, the smell of an office full of hatred each morning, no simple hatred, not for me only, but for the hated fact of an office, an elevator stuffed with the anger of elevator at 8 a.m. and 5 p.m., my voice on the telephone after nine months of office and elevator saying, I have to spend time on my dancing. Yes, I'm a dancer, it's my new career. Alone in the room after the phone crying at the weakness in my stomach. Dancer. This romance begins in a conversation off the top of my head, the kitchen at Grace Hospital is where it ends. Then the post office, here is escape at least from femininity, but not from the envy of colony, education, the list of insults is for this, better than, brighter than, richer than, beginning with this slender walk against the mountainous school. Each night, the black crowd of us parts in the cold darkness, smiling.

The truth is, well, truth is not important at one end of a
hemisphere where a bird dives close to you in an
ocean for a mouth full of fish, an ocean you come to
swim in every two years, you, a slave to your leaping
retina, capture the look of it. It is like saying you are
dead. This place so full of your absence, this place
you come to swim like habit, to taste like habit, this
place where you are a woman and your breasts need
armour to walk. Here. Nerve endings of steady light
pinpoint all. That litttle light trembling the water again,
that gray blue night pearl of the sea, the swirl of the
earth that dash water back and always forth, that
always fear of a woman watching the world from an
evening beach with her sister, the courage between
them to drink a beer and assume their presence
against the coralline chuckle of male voices. In
another place, not here, a woman might ... Our
nostalgia was a lie and the passage on that six hour
flight to ourselves is wide and like another world, and
then another one inside and is so separate and fast
to the skin but voiceless, never born, or born and
stilled ... hush.

In another place, not here, a woman might touch
something between beauty and nowhere, back there
and here, might pass hand over hand her own
trembling life, but I have tried to imagine a sea not
bleeding, a girl's glance full as a verse, a woman
growing old and never crying to a radio hissing of a
black boy's murder. I have tried to keep my throat
gurgling like a bird's. I have listened to the hard
gossip of race that inhabits this road. Even in this I
have tried to hum mud and feathers and sit peacefully
in this foliage of bones and rain. I have chewed a few
votive leaves here, their taste already disenchanting
my mothers. I have tried to write this thing calmly
even as its lines burn to a close. I have come to know
something simple. Each sentence realised or
dreamed jumps like a pulse with history and takes a
side. What I say in any language is told in faultless
knowledge of skin, in drunkenness and weeping,
told as a woman without matches and tinder, not in
words and in words and in words learned by heart,
told in secret and not in secret, and listen, does not
burn out or waste and is plenty and pitiless and loves.

hard against the soul

II

I want to wrap myself around you here in this line so
that you will know something, not just that I am dying
in some way but that I did this for some reason. This
grace, you see, come as a surprise and nothing till
now knock on my teeming skull, then, these warm
watery syllables, a woman's tongue so like a culture,
plunging toward stones not yet formed into flesh,
language not yet made ... I want to kiss you deeply,
smell, taste the warm water of your mouth as warm as
your hands. I lucky is grace that gather me up and
forgive my plainness.

III

She was a woman whose eyes came fresh, saying, I
trust you, you will not be the woman who walks out
into the Atlantic at Santa Maria and never returns.
You cannot dream this turquoise ocean enveloping
you in its murmuring thrall, your hands will not arrest
in the middle of gazing, you will not happen on an
easy thought like this in a hotel room in Guanabo, not
on a morning as you watch alone from this beach, the
sun dripping orange, or sitting on a marble bench in
Old Havana, vacantly. You will not look at your watch
on a night in early June and think this gentle sea as
good as any for a walk beyond the reflexes of your
flesh.

IV

you can hardly hear my voice now, woman,
but I heard you in my ear for many years to come
the pink tongue of a great shell murmuring and
yawning, muttering tea, wood, bread, she, blue,
stroking these simple names of habit, sweeter
and as common as night crumbling black flakes
of conversation to a sleep, repetitious as noons
and snow up north, the hoarse and throaty, I told you,
no milk, clean up ...

you can hardly hear my voice but I heard you
in my sleep big as waves reciting their prayers
so hourly the heart rocks to its real meaning,
saying, we must make a sense here to living,
this allegiance is as flesh to bone but older
and look, love, there are no poems to this only
triangles, scraps, prisons of purpled cloth,
time begins with these gestures, this
sudden silence needs words instead of whispering.

you can hardly hear my voice by now but woman
I felt your breath against my cheek in years to come
as losing my sight in night's black pause, I trace
the pearl of your sweat to morning, turning as you
turn, breasts to breasts mute prose we arc a leaping,
and no more may have passed here except
also the map to coming home, the tough geography
of trenches, quarrels, placards, barricades.

V

It is not sufficient here to mark the skin's water or fold,
the back soft, the neck secret, the lips purpled. She
startled me just last night. I heard her singing and
could not dance. I heard her navigate the thick soil of
who we are. Her boundless black self rising,
honeying.

for faith

VI

listen, just because I've spent these
few verses fingering this register of the heart,
clapping life, as a woman on a noisy beach,
calling blood into veins dry as sand,
do not think that things escape me,
this drawn skin of hunger twanging as a bow,
this shiver whistling into the white face of capital, a
shadow traipsing, icy veined and bloodless through
city alleys of wet light, the police bullet glistening
through a black woman's spine in November, against
red pools of democracy bursting the hemisphere's
seams, the heart sinks, and sinks like a moon.

VII

still I must say something here
something that drives this verse into the future,
not where I go loitering in my sleep,
not where the eyes brighten every now and again
on old scores, now I must step sprightly. I dreamless.

VIII

but here, at this spot, all I see is the past
at the museum of the revolution in old Havana when I
should be looking at the bullet hole in Fidel's
camisole or the skirt that Haydee Santamaria wore in
prison, I see a coffle just as I turn, about to leave,
toward my left, toward the future, the woman sitting at
the door black and historic saying to herself this is
only white history, a coffle, shining still after this long
time, new as day under my eyes. I spun in that room,
my voice said *oh dear*, as if I'd only spilt water, *oh
god*, as if my skin had just rubbed this iron silvery with
sweat.

IX

look, I know you went searching on the beach
for my body last night and maybe you will find it
there, one day, but I'll tell you now, it will be on this
beach, or a beach such as this where they made a
revolution, and it will be near that dune where you
oiled your skin darkly against the sun and it will be
because I am not good enough, not the woman to live
in the world we are fighting to make and it will be on a
day like the one when you bought rum for Marta
Beatriz because she said she loved women and you
wanted to believe her, it will be like how we walked
from Marazul to Boca Ciega climbing over the sand
covering the road and after I spend three days
showing you mimosa running and you finally see it.

X

Then it is this simple. I felt the unordinary romance of
women who love women for the first time. It burst in
my mouth. Someone said this is your first lover, you
will never want to leave her. I had it in mind that I
would be an old woman with you. But perhaps I
always had it in mind simply to be an old woman,
darkening, somewhere with another old woman,
then, I decided it was you when you found me in that
apartment drinking whisky for breakfast. When I came
back from Grenada and went crazy for two years, that
time when I could hear anything and my skin was
flaming like a nerve and the walls were like paper
and my eyes could not close. I suddenly sensed you
at the end of my room waiting. I saw your back arched
against this city we inhabit like guerillas, I brushed my
hand, conscious, against your soft belly, waking up.

I saw this woman once in another poem, sitting,
throwing water over her head on the rind of a country
beach as she turned toward her century. Seeing her
no part of me was comfortable with itself. I envied her,
so old and set aside, a certain habit washed from her
eyes. I must have recognized her. I know I watched
her along the rim of the surf promising myself, an old
woman is free. In my nerves something there
unravelling, and she was a place to go, believe me,
against gales of masculinity but in that then, she was
masculine, old woman, old bird squinting at the
water's wing above her head, swearing under her
breath. I had a mind that she would be graceful in me
and she might have been if I had not heard you
laughing in another tense and lifted my head from her
dry charm.

You ripped the world open for me. Someone said this is your first lover you will never want to leave her. My lips cannot say old woman darkening anymore, she is the peace of another life that didn't happen and couldn't happen in my flesh and wasn't peace but flight into old woman, prayer, to the saints of my ancestry, the gourd and bucket carrying women who stroke their breasts into stone shedding offspring and smile. I know since that an old woman, darkening, cuts herself away limb from limb, sucks herself white, running, skin torn and raw like a ball of bright light, flying, into old woman. I only know now that my longing for this old woman was longing to leave the prisoned gaze of men.

It's true, you spend the years after thirty turning over
the suggestion that you have been an imbecile,
hearing finally all the words that passed you like air,
like so much fun, or all the words that must have
existed while you were listening to others. What
would I want with this sentence you say flinging it
aside ... and then again sometimes you were duped,
poems placed deliberately in your way. At eleven, the
strophe of a yellow dress sat me crosslegged in my
sex. It was a boy's abrupt birthday party. A yellow
dress for a tomboy, the ritual stab of womanly gathers
at the waist. *She look like a boy in a dress*, my big
sister say, a lyric and feminine correction from a
watchful aunt, *don't say that, she look nice and pretty.*
Nice and pretty, laid out to splinter you, so that never,
until it is almost so late as not to matter do you grasp
some part, something missing like a wing, some
fragment of your real self.

Old woman, that was the fragment that I caught in
your eye, that was the look I fell in love with, the piece
of you that you kept, the piece of you left, the lesbian,
the inviolable, sitting on a beach in a time that did not
hear your name or else it would have thrown you into
the sea, or you, hear that name yourself and walked
willingly into the muting blue. Instead you sat and I
saw your look and pursued one eye until it came to
the end of itself and then I saw the other,
the blazing fragment.

Someone said this is your first lover, you will never
want to leave her. There are saints of this ancestry
too who laugh themselves like jamettes in the
pleasure of their legs and caress their sex in mirrors.
I have become myself. A woman who looks
at a woman and says, here, I have found you,
in this, I am blackening in my way. You ripped the
world raw. It was as if another life exploded in my
face, brightening, so easily the brow of a wing
touching the surf, so easily I saw my own body, that
is, my eyes followed me to myself, touched myself
as a place, another life, terra. They say this place
does not exist, then, my tongue is mythic. I was here
before.

Dionne Brand is a Toronto writer. She was born in the Caribbean and has lived in Toronto for the past 20 years. She studied English and Philosophy at the University of Toronto, has an M.A. in Philosophy of Education and is working on a Ph.D. in Women's History.

Brand has published five books of poetry – *'Fore day morning, Earth Magic* (children's poetry), *Winter Epigrams* and *Epigrams to Ernesto Cardenal in Defense of Claudia, Primitive Offensive,* and, *Chronicles of the Hostile Sun.* Her poems and other writing have appeared in Fireweed, Prism, This Magazine, Canadian Women's Studies, Fuse, and Poetry Canada Review where her columns on Caribbean poetry also appeared. She has also co-authored a work of non-fiction, *Rivers Have Sources Trees Have Roots-Speaking of Racism.* Her first book of short stories, *Sans Souci and Other Stories,* was published in 1988.

Her poetry is included in various anthologies including the *Penguin Book of Caribbean Verse* and *Poetry by Canadian Women* – Oxford University Press, Toronto. Also a writer of short stories, her work is included in the anthology *Stories by Canadian Women* – Oxford University Press, Toronto.

Brand has read her work at numerous public readings across Canada, doing a stint as a writer-in-residence at the Halifax City Regional Library. She was poetry teacher at the West Coast Women and Words Society Summer School and Retreat in 1988.

She is the associate director and writer of the NFB Studio D documentary *Older, Stronger, Wiser,* and is currently working as director of a second documentary, *Sisters in the Struggle.* She is presently writer-in-residence at the University of Toronto, 1990-1991.

Seen through the press by Libby Scheier
Cover design: Stephanie Power / Reactor
Cover art: Grace Channer
Text design: Nelson Adams
Typeset in Century
Printed in Canada

Coach House Press
401 (rear) Huron Street
Toronto, Canada M5S 2G5